Smith

Amazing Earth

Courtney Acampora

Contents

Amazing Earth

Earth is an amazing planet.

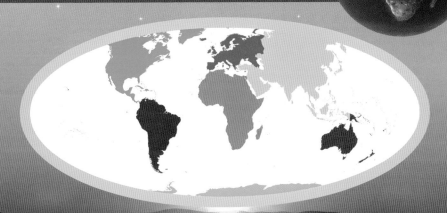

Earth is made up of seven **continents**. Each continent is **unique**.

North America

North America is a continent.

It includes the United States, Canada, and Mexico.

Canada

United States

Mexico

North America has mountains. It has deserts and beaches.

The Grand Canyon

The Grand Canyon is in Arizona.
It was formed by the Colorado River.
It is millions of years old.

The Grand Canyon has amazing sights.

North America

Denali

Denali is in Alaska.

It is the highest mountain in North America.
Denali was called "Mount McKinley" until 2015.

Carlsbad Caverns

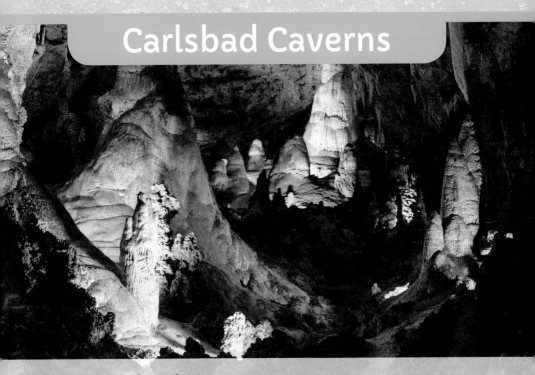

The Carlsbad Caverns are caves.
They are underground in New Mexico.
They were created millions of years ago.
The caves were once part of an ocean!

South America

South America is a large continent. It is connected to North America.

South America has rainforests. South America has many interesting **cultures**.

Angel Falls

Angel Falls is in Venezuela.
It is the highest waterfall in the world.
It was named after Jimmie Angel.
Jimmie Angel was an American aviator.
He saw the waterfall from a plane in 1933.

South America

The Amazon Rainforest

The Amazon is a giant rainforest. It is a **habitat** full of plants and animals. It has more wildlife than anywhere else on Earth.

Atacama Desert

The Atacama Desert is in Chile.
It looks similar to the planet Mars.
New space **technology** is tested there.

Europe

Europe has forty-four countries.
Europe has many manmade landmarks.

It has many landscapes such as
mountains, beaches, and **tundra**.

Reindeer Migration

Thousands of reindeer **migrate** from Norway to Finland.
They travel across the ice.
They feed on grasses in the summer.
The reindeer travel to a new home each winter.

Europe

White Cliffs of Dover

The White Cliffs are in England.
They are white from seashells and sea creatures.
They were formed millions of years ago.
The cliffs are ten miles long.

Iceland Volcanoes

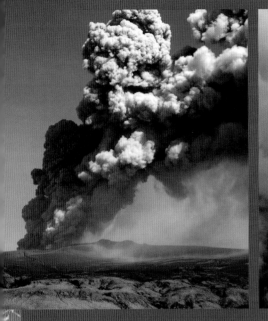

Iceland is home to fire and ice.
Iceland has one hundred and thirty active and inactive volcanoes.
In 2010, a big volcano erupted in Iceland.
It is also home to the largest **glacier** in Europe.

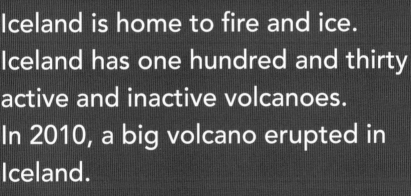

Africa

Africa is a large continent.

The Sahara Desert is in the north.
The Nile River is located in Africa.
Many animals live in Africa.

Massive Migration

The Serengeti is a savanna.
A savanna is a grassland.

Wildebeest, zebras, and gazelles migrate
in the savanna.
They head north in the spring.
They head south in the fall.

Africa

The Nile River

The Nile is the longest river on Earth.
It is located in Egypt.
The Nile River is an important source of water.

Mount Kilimanjaro

Mount Kilimanjaro is a large mountain.
It is known as the "Roof of Africa."
The mountain is made of volcanoes.
It was formed around a million years ago.

Asia

Asia is the largest continent in the world.

Asia has deserts, tundra, and tropical beaches.
It is also home to two-thirds of the people on Earth.

Mount Everest

Mount Everest is the tallest mountain above sea level.
It is in the Himalayas.
It slowly grows taller each year.

The Dead Sea

The Dead Sea is in the Middle East.
The Dead Sea isn't a sea.
It is a lake.
The Dead Sea is full of salt.
Plants and animals can't live in such salty water.

Gobi Desert

The Gobi Desert is a cold desert.
It is located in central Asia.
It can be minus forty degrees
Fahrenheit.
The Gobi Desert is mostly rock.

Antarctica

Antarctica is at the bottom of the planet.

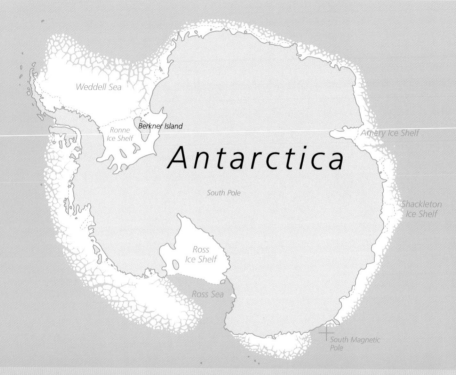

Weddell Sea

Ronne
Ice Shelf

Berkner Island

Amery Ice Shelf

Antarctica

South Pole

Shackleton
Ice Shelf

Ross
Ice Shelf

Ross Sea

South Magnetic
Pole

It is cold and icy there.
Antarctica is always covered by a
thick layer of ice.
The ice never melts completely.

Australia

Australia is the smallest continent.
Australia is a continent and a country.
Australia has many unique animals.
They are found nowhere else in the world.

The Great Barrier Reef

The Great Barrier Reef is a large coral reef.
It is the largest living structure in the world.
It can be seen from space.
It is home to twenty-five percent of ocean life on earth.

Australia

The Outback

The Outback is a large, dry region.
It takes up most of Australia.
Uluru (Ayers Rock) is in the Outback.
It is a giant sandstone.

Earth is home to many unique sites.
Earth has volcanoes, coral reefs, and
much more.
Earth is an amazing planet!

Amazing Earth QUIZ

1. How many continents does Earth have?
   a) Five
   b) Ten
   c) Seven

2. What formed the Grand Canyon?
   a) An earthquake
   b) The Colorado River
   c) The Pacific Ocean

3. Why are the White Cliffs at Dover white?
   a) From volcanic ash
   b) From seashells and sea creatures
   c) From quartz, a type of rock

4. What is the tallest mountain above sea level on Earth?
   a) Mount Everest
   b) Denali
   c) Mount Kilimanjaro

5. Which continent is the largest?
   a) Asia
   b) North America
   c) Africa

6. What is so big it can be seen from space?
   a) The Outback
   b) The Amazon Rainforest
   c) The Great Barrier Reef

GLOSSARY

Continents: seven large landmasses on Earth

Culture: customs and beliefs of a group of people

Glacier: a large mass of slow-moving ice

Habitat: place where plants and animals live

 **Migrate:** move from one habitat to another

Technology: machines and equipment developed to solve problems

Tundra: Arctic region with  frozen soil and no trees

Unique: the one and only of its kind

The Grand Canyon

Angel Falls

Mount Kilimanjaro

White Cliffs of Dover

Great Barrier Reef

Amazon Rainforest

Angel Falls is the largest waterfall in the world.

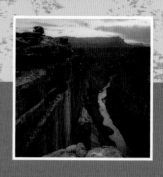

The Grand Canyon is in Arizona. It is millions of years old.

Ancient skeletons of sea creatures make up the White Cliffs of Dover.

Mount Kilimanjaro is a large mountain that means "roof of Africa."

The Amazon Rainforest has more wildlife than anywhere else.

The Great Barrier Reef is the largest coral reef in the world.

PRE-LEVEL 1: ASPIRING READERS

• Basic factual texts with familiar themes and content

• Concepts in text are reinforced by photos

• Includes glossary to reinforce reading comprehension

• Phonic regularity

• Simple sentence structure and repeated sentence patterns

• Easy vocabulary familiar to kindergarteners and first-graders

LEVEL 2: DEVELOPING READERS

LEVEL 3: ENGAGED READERS

LEVEL 4: FLUENT READERS

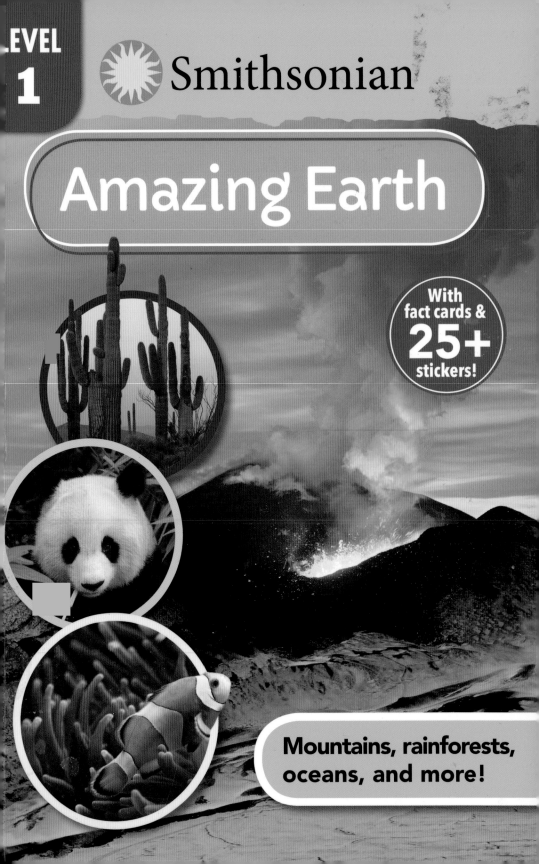

LEVEL 1

Smithsonian

Amazing Earth

With fact cards & **25+** stickers!

Mountains, rainforests, oceans, and more!